ADVENT *with* POPE FRANCIS

D1440964

ADVENT *with* POPE FRANCIS

DAILY REFLECTIONS AND PRAYERS

Edited by

Marianne Lorraine Trouvé, FSP

Pauline
BOOKS & MEDIA

Boston

Library of Congress Control Number: 2015946717
CIP data is available.

ISBN 10: 0-8198-0845-8

ISBN 13: 978-0-8198-0845-5

Excerpts from Pope Francis' audiences, homilies, angelus messages, addresses, messages and exhortations copyright © Libreria Editrice Vaticana. Used with permission.

Unless otherwise noted, the Scripture quotations contained herein are taken directly from Pope Francis' works.

All other Scripture quotations contained herein are from the *New Revised Standard Version Bible: Catholic Edition,* copyright © 1989, 1993, Division of Christian Education of the National Council of the Churches of Christ in the United States of America. Used by permission. All rights reserved.

Compiled and with reflection questions and prayers by the Daughters of St. Paul.

Cover design by Rosana Usselmann

Cover photo © Stefano Spaziani

Published by Pauline Books & Media, 50 Saint Paul's Avenue, Boston, MA 02130–3491

Printed in the U.S.A.

www.pauline.org

Pauline Books & Media is the publishing house of the Daughters of St. Paul, an international congregation of women religious serving the Church with the communications media.

1 2 3 4 5 6 7 8 9   19 18 17 16 15

Contents

APPENDIX II

WEEK 1

A Journey of Joy

Our Journey to Meet with Jesus

In days to come
the mountain of the LORD's house
shall be established as the highest of the mountains. . . .
Many peoples shall come and say,
"Come, let us go up to the mountain of the LORD,
to the house of the God of Jacob;
that he may teach us his ways
and that we may walk in his paths."

—Isaiah 2:2–3

The Prophet Isaiah speaks to us about a journey, and he says that in the latter days, at the end of the journey, the mountain of the Lord's temple shall be established as the highest mountain. He says this to tell us that our life is a journey: we must go on this journey to arrive at the mountain of the Lord, to encounter Jesus. The most important thing that can happen to a person is to meet Jesus—this encounter with Jesus who loves us, who has saved us, who has given his life for us. Encounter Jesus. And we are journeying in order to meet Jesus.

We could ask ourselves this question: But when do I meet Jesus? Only at the end? No, no! We meet him every day. How? In prayer, when you pray, you meet Jesus. When you receive Communion, you meet Jesus in the sacraments.

Homily, December 1, 2013

REFLECTION

Where am I on my journey to meet Jesus? How can I meet him today?

PRAYER

Jesus, I long for you to come into my life. Help me to be watchful and alert to the signs of your presence.

Meeting Jesus with Faith

O house of Jacob,
come, let us walk
in the light of the LORD!

—Isaiah 2:5

The Lord marveled at the centurion. He marveled at his faith. The centurion made a journey to meet the Lord, but he made it in faith. He not only encountered the Lord, but he came to know the joy of being encountered by him. And this is precisely the sort of encounter we desire, the encounter of faith; to encounter the Lord, but also to allow ourselves to be encountered by him. . . . In the prayer at the beginning of Mass, we asked for the grace to make this journey with several dispositions that will aid us—perseverance in prayer: to pray more; diligence in fraternal charity: to draw closer to those in need; and joy in praising the Lord. Let us begin this journey in prayer, charity, and praise, so that the Lord might come to meet us, but let us allow him to meet us with our defenses down, in openness!

Homily, December 2, 2013

REFLECTION

In what practical way can I make prayer a vital part of my Advent journey?

PRAYER

Lord, I believe in you. Strengthen my lack of faith!

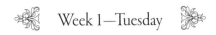

The Joy of Knowing Jesus

At that same hour Jesus rejoiced in the Holy Spirit and said, "I thank you, Father, Lord of heaven and earth, because you have hidden these things from the wise and the intelligent and have revealed them to infants; yes, Father, for such was your gracious will."

—Luke 10:21

Jesus was full of joy. . . . His inner joy comes precisely from this relationship with the Father in the Holy Spirit. And this is the joy he gives to us, and this joy is true peace. It is not a static, quiet, tranquil peace; Christian peace is a joyful peace. . . . A Church without joy is unthinkable, since Jesus has desired that his bride, the Church, be joyful. The joy of the Church is to announce the name of Jesus. . . . The peace of which Isaiah speaks is a peace full of joy, a peace of praise, a peace—we might say—that is loud with praise, a peace that bears fruit in becoming a mother of new children, a peace that comes precisely from the joy of praising the Trinity, and from evangelization, of going out to people to tell them who Jesus is.

Homily, December 3, 2013

REFLECTION

How can I radiate to others the joy that comes from Jesus?

PRAYER

Jesus, as I wait for your coming anew into my heart at Christmas, fill me with the joy of your presence and help me to share it with those around me.

The Banquet of the Lord

On this mountain the LORD of hosts will make
for all peoples
a feast of rich food, a feast of well-aged wines . . .

—Isaiah 25:6

Besides physical hunger, man experiences another hunger, a hunger that cannot be satiated with ordinary food. It's a hunger for life, a hunger for love, a hunger for eternity. And the sign of *manna . . .* contains in itself this dimension: it was the symbol of a food that satisfies this deep human hunger. Jesus gives us this food, rather, *he himself* is *the living bread* that gives life to the world (see Jn 6:51). His Body is the true food in the form of bread; his Blood is the true drink in the form of wine. It isn't simple nourishment to satisfy the body, like manna; the Body of Christ is the bread of the last times, capable of giving life, eternal life, because this bread is made of love. The Eucharist communicates the Lord's love for us, a love so great that it nourishes us with himself.

Homily, June 19, 2014

Reflection

The Eucharist, the Bread of Life, gives us a pledge of eternal life. Jesus is truly present in the Eucharist. What difference can that make in my life?

Prayer

Jesus, thank you for the gift you have given us of yourself in the Eucharist.

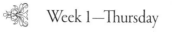

Week 1—Thursday

Put on Christ

Trust in the Lord forever,
for in the Lord God
you have an everlasting rock.

—Isaiah 26:4

"Put on faith," and life will take on a new flavor; life will have a compass to show you the way. "Put on hope," and every one of your days will be enlightened and your horizon will no longer be dark, but luminous. "Put on love," and your life will be like a house built on rock; your journey will be joyful, because you will find many friends to journey with you. Put on faith, put on hope, put on love!

. . . "Put on Christ" in your lives. . . . Christ awaits you in his word; listen carefully to him and his presence will arouse your heart. "Put on Christ": he awaits you in the sacrament of Penance; with his mercy he will cure all the wounds caused by sin. Do not be afraid to ask God's forgiveness because he never tires of forgiving us, like a father who loves us.

Homily in Copacabana, Brazil, July 25, 2013

REFLECTION

What are some practical ways I can "put on Christ" in my life?

PRAYER

Jesus, no matter what happens, I trust in you and your loving providence in my life.

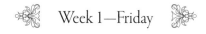

Knock at the Door

Out of their gloom and darkness
the eyes of the blind shall see.

—Isaiah 29:18

The blind men who entered Jericho cried aloud, and the Lord's friends wanted them to be silent. [Yet the blind men] ask the Lord for a grace . . . "But do it! It's my right that you do this!" Here, crying aloud is a sign of prayer. Perhaps this sounds rather bad, but praying is a little like bothering God so that he listens to us. . . . Jesus tells us: "Ask!" and he also says: "Knock at the door!" and whoever knocks at the door makes noise; he disturbs, he bothers. . . . This is also the way the needy pray in the Gospel. . . . the blind feel confident in asking the Lord to make them well. So much so that the Lord asks them: "Do you believe that I am able to do this?" to which they respond, "Yes, Lord. We believe! We are sure!'"

Homily, December 6, 2013

REFLECTION

How strongly do I believe that God will hear and answer my prayer? Do I also allow God to change my heart so that my requests are more in line with his desires?

PRAYER

Jesus, enlighten the eyes of my heart. Help me to believe that when I pray, even if I don't get what I want, I will get exactly what I need.

Word and Light

"As you go, proclaim the good news...."

—Matthew 10:7

Those who have opened their hearts to God's love, heard his voice and received his light, cannot keep this gift to themselves. Since faith is hearing and seeing, it is also handed on as word and light.... Saint Paul used these two very images. On the one hand he says: "But just as we have the same spirit of faith that is in accordance with Scripture—'I believed, and so I spoke'—we also believe, and so we speak" (2 Cor 4:13). The word, once accepted, becomes a response, a confession of faith, which spreads to others and invites them to believe. Paul also uses the image of light: "All of us, with unveiled faces, seeing the glory of the Lord as though reflected in a mirror, are being transformed into the same image" (2 Cor 3:18).

Light of Faith, no. 37

REFLECTION

How can I speak in a way that reflects the light of faith? Do I know how to proclaim the Good News even without words?

PRAYER

Jesus, you are the light of the world. Help me to think, speak, and act in ways that spread your love and your light.

The Immaculate Conception of Mary

Blessed be the God and Father of our Lord Jesus Christ, who has blessed us in Christ with every spiritual blessing in the heavenly places . . .

—Ephesians 1:3

Regarding this love, this mercy, the divine grace poured into our hearts, one single thing is asked in return: unreserved giving. None of us can buy salvation! Salvation is a free gift of the Lord. . . . As we have received freely, so are we called to give freely (see Mt 10:8), imitating Mary, who, immediately upon receiving the angel's announcement, went to share the gift of her fruitfulness with her relative Elizabeth. Because if everything has been given to us, then everything must be passed on. How? By allowing the Holy Spirit to make of us a gift for others. The Spirit is a gift for us and we, by the power of the Spirit, must be a gift for others and allow the Holy Spirit to turn us into instruments of acceptance, instruments of reconciliation, instruments of forgiveness

Angelus, December 8, 2014

Reflection

Mary was chosen to play a special role in God's plan of salvation. Through Baptism I too have been chosen. What is my role and how have I fulfilled it thus far?

Prayer

Mary, my Mother, intercede for me that I might correspond to grace just as you did. Help me to say "yes" to God's invitation to be an apostle.

WEEK 2

God Consoles Us

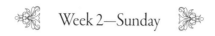
The Fire of Hope

"Here is your God!"
See, the LORD GOD comes with might . . .

—Isaiah 40:9–10

Today there is need for people to be witnesses to the mercy and tenderness of God, who spurs the resigned, enlivens the disheartened, ignites the fire of hope. He ignites the fire of hope! We don't. So many situations require our comforting witness, [require us] to be joyful, comforting people. I am thinking of those who are burdened by suffering, injustice, and tyranny; of those who are slaves to money, to power, to success, to worldliness. . . . They have fabricated consolation, not the true comfort of the Lord! We are all called to comfort our brothers and sisters, to testify that God alone can eliminate the causes of existential and spiritual tragedies. He can do it! He is powerful!

Angelus, December 7, 2014

REFLECTION

In what ways can I comfort those persons in my life who are suffering?

PRAYER

Holy Spirit, you are the Comforter. Be with me and with those who most need your comfort today.

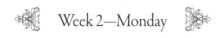

The Merciful Love of Jesus

"Friend, your sins are forgiven you."

—Luke 5:20

When I go to confession, it is in order to be healed, to heal my soul, to heal my heart and to be healed of some wrongdoing. . . . When we have gone to confession with a soul weighed down and with a little sadness, when we receive Jesus' forgiveness we feel at peace, with that peace of soul that is so beautiful, which only Jesus can give, only him. . . . When one finishes confession one leaves free, grand, beautiful, forgiven, candid, happy. This is the beauty of confession! I would like to ask you . . . when was the last time you made your confession? . . . And if much time has passed, do not lose another day. Go; the priest will be good. Jesus is there, and Jesus is more benevolent than priests. Jesus receives you; he receives you with so much love.

General Audience, February 19, 2014

REFLECTION

In the sacrament of Penance we not only receive forgiveness of our sins, but also the special graces we need to avoid sin in the future. How can I take better advantage of this marvelous opportunity for spiritual growth?

PRAYER

Jesus, I trust in your mercy and love.

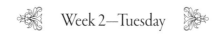
The Lord Comforts His People

Comfort, O comfort my people,
says your God.

—Isaiah 40:1

The Lord consoles us with tenderness. The Lord, the great God, is not afraid of tenderness. He becomes tenderness, he becomes a baby, he makes himself little. In the Gospel, Jesus says: "It is the will of my Father in heaven that not one of these little ones should perish" (Mt 18:14). . . . Each one of us is very, very important to the Lord.

Jesus consoled the disciples, drawing near them to console them, to give them hope, drawing near to them with tenderness. Let us think of the tenderness he showed to the apostles, to Mary Magdalene, to the disciples on the road to Emmaus. . . . Do not be afraid of the Lord's consolation; do not be afraid of being open, of asking for it, of searching for it, for it is that consolation that gives us hope and makes us feel the tenderness of God the Father.

Homily, December 10, 2013

REFLECTION

If life has been getting burdensome, how can I turn to the Lord and receive his consolation?

PRAYER

Thank you, Lord, for the tenderness and love you show me. Help me to keep going despite the trials of life, and to trust in you with great hope.

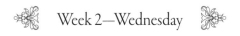

Give Comfort to Others

Those who wait for the LORD shall renew their
strength,
they shall mount up with wings like eagles,
they shall run and not be weary,
they shall walk and not faint.

—Isaiah 40:31

Jesus promises to give rest to everyone, but he also gives us an invitation, which is like a commandment: "Take my yoke upon you, and learn from me; for I am gentle and lowly in heart" (Mt 11:29). The "yoke" of the Lord consists of taking on the burden of others with fraternal love. Once Christ's comfort and rest is received, we are called in turn to become rest and comfort for our brothers and sisters, with a docile and humble attitude, in imitation of the Teacher. Docility and humility of heart help us not only to take on the burden of others, but also to keep our personal views, our judgments, our criticism, or our indifference from weighing on them. Let us invoke Mary Most Holy, who welcomes under her mantle all the tired and worn-out people. . . .

Angelus, July 6, 2014

REFLECTION

How can I reach out to others during this Advent, especially the poor and those in greater need?

PRAYER

Jesus, you told us that whatever we do to others, we do to you. Help me to see you in those who are in need, and to reach out to them in whatever ways I can.

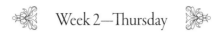

Week 2—Thursday

The Beauty of Silence

"Let anyone with ears listen!"

—Matthew 11:15

I have always been struck by the Lord's encounter with Elijah, when the Lord speaks with Elijah. He was on the mountain when he saw the Lord pass by, "not in the hail, in the rain, in the storm, in the wind. . . . The Lord was in the still soft breeze" (see 1 Kings 19:11–13). This is the music of the Lord's language. As we prepare for Christmas, we should listen to it. It will do us great, great good. Normally Christmas is a loud feast, so it will do us good to be silent a little, in order to listen to these words of love, of great closeness, these words of tenderness. We need to be silent during this season so that, as the preface says, we might vigilantly keep watch.

Homily, December 12, 2013

REFLECTION

In the rush of Christmas preparations, how can I find some time and space to listen in silence to the Lord's words of love?

PRAYER

Jesus, don't let me get so caught up in getting gifts for others that I forget to prepare my heart to receive the greatest gift—you!

The Light of Faith

I am the LORD your God,
who teaches you for your own good . . .

—Isaiah 48:17

Faith is a light, for once the flame of faith dies out, all other lights begin to dim. The light of faith is unique, since it is capable of illuminating *every aspect* of human existence. A light this powerful cannot come from ourselves but from a more primordial source: in a word, it must come from God. Faith is born of an encounter with the living God who calls us and reveals his love, a love which precedes us and upon which we can lean for security and for building our lives.

Transformed by this love, we gain fresh vision, new eyes to see; we realize that it contains a great promise of fulfillment, and that a vision of the future opens up before us. Faith, received from God as a supernatural gift, becomes a light for our way, guiding our journey through time.

Light of Faith, no. 4

REFLECTION

How does my faith affect the way I view life and its events? How can I grow in faith so that it makes a real difference in my life?

PRAYER

Jesus, thank you for the gift of faith and for the light it brings to the problems of life. May my faith be a lighted lamp to guide me closer to you.

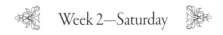
When the Promise Seems Distant

Then we will never turn back from you . . .

—Psalm 80:18

John [the Baptist's] most difficult milestone, because the Lord had ways that he hadn't imagined, was to suffer not only the darkness of the cell but the darkness of his heart. "But is he the one? Have I made a mistake?" John sent his disciples to Jesus to ask him: "Are you he who is to come, or shall we look for another?" . . . John's humiliation is twofold: the humiliation of his death, as the price of a whim, [and the humiliation of not being able to glimpse] the history of salvation: the humiliation of the darkness of the spirit. John now sees Jesus far away.

That promise has become distant. And he ends up alone, in the dark, in humiliation . . . so that the Lord would increase.

Homily, June 24, 2014

REFLECTION

At some point in the Advent journey the promise of Christ may seem distant. It may be easy to wonder: "What difference will it really make?" If that happens, it can help to recall a time when God's presence lifted me up.

PRAYER

Even though your promise may seem distant, Jesus, I trust that in your own good time you will bring me the graces and gifts that I long for.

WEEK 3

Hope in the Lord

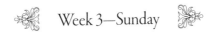

Jesus Is Our Joy

Rejoice in the Lord always.

—Philippians 4:4

The human heart desires joy. We all desire joy, for every family, every people aspires to happiness. But what is the joy that the Christian is called to live out and bear witness to? It is the joy that comes from the *closeness of God*, from his *presence* in our life. From the moment Jesus entered history, with his birth in Bethlehem, humanity received the seed of the Kingdom of God, like the soil receives the seed, the promise of a future harvest. There is no need to look further! Jesus has come to bring joy to all people for all time. It is not just a hopeful joy or a joy postponed until paradise, as if here on earth we are sad but in paradise we will be filled with joy. No! It is not that, but a joy already real and tangible now, because *Jesus himself is our joy*, and with Jesus joy finds its home ...

Angelus, December 14, 2014

REFLECTION

In what ways can I reflect to others the joy that Jesus brings?

PRAYER

Fill me with joy, Lord, so that I may praise and glorify your name.

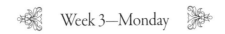
The Promises of God

"The oracle of Balaam son of Beor . . .
the oracle of one who hears the words of God . . ."

—Numbers 24:3–4

Thisis the prophet, a man whose eyes are opened, and who hears and speaks the words of God, who knows how to see into the moment and to go forward into the future. But first he has listened; he has heard the word of God [and holds] these three moments within himself. The past: the prophet is aware of the promise and he holds God's promise in his heart; he keeps it alive; he remembers it; he repeats it. He then looks into the present: he looks at his people and he experiences the power of the spirit to speak a word to them that will lift them up, to continue their journey toward the future. The prophet is a man of three times: the promise of the past, the contemplation of the present, the courage to point out the path toward the future.

Homily, December 16, 2013

Reflection

A promise carries with it a hope of fulfillment. How does hope in God's promises enrich my daily life?

Prayer

Jesus, give me a strong hope that never goes dim even in times of darkness.

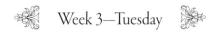
Trust in the Lord

*For I will leave in the midst of you
a people humble and lowly.*

—Zephaniah 3:12

The three characteristics of the faithful People of God are humility, poverty, and trust in the Lord. This is the path of salvation. . . . Each one of us can say: "Lord, I offer you my sins, the only thing that we can offer you." . . . We can say: "Lord, these are my sins; they aren't this man's or that woman's. . . . They're mine. You take them. This way I'll be saved." When we are able to do this, then we will be that beautiful people—"the humble and poor people"—who trust in the name of the Lord.

Homily, December 16, 2014

REFLECTION

At certain moments the reality of our sins might make us tremble. How can we make up for them? We can't, but Jesus can. That is why he came to be our Savior.

PRAYER

Lord Jesus, I trust in you as my Savior. Do not let me either gloss over my sins or slide into despair over them, for in you I hope!

Bring People to Jesus Christ

"Are you the one who is to come, or are we to wait for another?"

—Luke 7:20

We who are baptized, children of the Church, are called to accept ever anew the presence of God among us and to help others to discover him, or to rediscover what they have forgotten. It is a most beautiful mission, like that of John the Baptist: to direct the people to Christ—not to ourselves!—for he is the destination to which the human heart tends when it seeks joy and happiness. . . . Jesus is the Word of God who today continues to illuminate the path of humanity; his gestures—the sacraments—are the manifestation of the tenderness, consolation, and love that the Father bears for every human being.

Angelus, December 14, 2014

REFLECTION

John the Baptist sought assurance from Jesus that he indeed was the Messiah. Jesus pointed to the evidence: "The blind see, the deaf hear. . . ." God sometimes works in dramatic ways in our lives, and at other times his work might be hard to detect. If someone is discouraged, can I help that person to see what God is doing in his or her life?

PRAYER

Jesus, open my eyes that I may see, and open my ears that I may hear. Help me to focus on you in order to bring to others the joy of the Gospel.

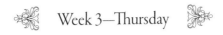 Week 3—Thursday

The Mercy of God

My steadfast love shall not depart from you . . .
says the LORD, *who has compassion on you.*

—Isaiah 54:10

J esus' reminder urges each of us never to stop at the
surface of things, especially when we have a person
before us. We are called to look beyond, *to focus on the*
heart in order to see how much generosity everyone is
capable of. No one can be excluded from the mercy of
God; everyone knows the way to access it. The Church is
the *house where everyone is welcomed and no one is*
rejected. Her doors remain wide open, so that those who
are touched by grace may find the assurance of

forgiveness. The greater the sin, the greater the love that must be shown by the Church to those who repent. With how much love Jesus looks at us! With how much love he heals our sinful heart!

Homily, March 13, 2015

REFLECTION

Have I let Jesus into my heart to heal my wounds?

PRAYER

Jesus, I trust you. Please come into my heart and fill it with your love.

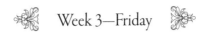

Faith Lights Our Way

He testified to the truth.

—John 5:33

In God's gift of faith, a supernatural infused virtue, we realize that a great love has been offered us, a good word has been spoken to us, and that when we welcome that word—Jesus Christ the Word made flesh—the Holy Spirit transforms us, lights up our way to the future, and enables us joyfully to advance along that way on wings of hope. Thus wonderfully interwoven, faith, hope, and charity are the driving forces of the Christian life as it advances toward full communion with God.

Light of Faith, no. 7

REFLECTION

The Holy Spirit sends us inspirations to help us follow Jesus better. How do I respond to them?

PRAYER

Holy Spirit, come into my heart and transform it so that I may always welcome the Word of God.

WEEK 4

The Lord Is Near

A Note for the Fourth Week of Advent

From December 17 to 24, the weekday liturgical texts are arranged by date, not by the day of the week. For Saturday of Week 3, see the meditation for the proper date.

Recognize God's Time

"Do not be afraid, Mary, for you have found favor with God."

—Luke 1:30

The Mother of Christ [knew how] to *recognize God's time*. Mary made possible the Incarnation of the Son of God . . . thanks to her humble and brave "yes." Mary teaches us to seize the right moment when Jesus comes into our life and asks for a ready and generous answer. And Jesus is coming. Indeed, the mystery of the birth of Jesus in Bethlehem took place historically more than 2,000 years ago but occurs as a spiritual event in the "today" of the liturgy. The Word, who found a home in the virgin womb of Mary, comes in the celebration of Christmas to knock once again at the heart of every Christian. . . . Each of us is called to respond, like Mary, with a personal and sincere "yes," placing oneself fully at the disposal of God and of his mercy, of his love.

Angelus, December 21, 2014

REFLECTION

Am I, like Mary, ready to open the door of my heart when Jesus knocks?

PRAYER

Jesus, I want to welcome you into my heart!

 December 17

God Makes History with Us

An account of the genealogy of Jesus the Messiah, the son of David, the son of Abraham.

—Matthew 1:1

God had this idea: to make the journey with us. He called Abraham . . . and he invited him to walk. Abraham began the journey: he begot Isaac, and Isaac begot Jacob, and Jacob begot Judah. God journeys with his people because he did not want to come and save us apart from history; he wants to make history with us.

It is a history wrought of holiness and sin. . . . The genealogy of Jesus is filled with saints and sinners: from

Abraham and David, who converted after his sin, two high caliber sinners, who sinned gravely. But God made history with them all. . . . This is beautiful: God makes history with us.

Homily, December 17, 2013

REFLECTION

What does my personal history with the Lord teach me about his love for me?

PRAYER

Lord, I praise and thank you for the wonderful way you have worked in my life!

 December 18

God Helps Us in Our Trials

When Joseph awoke from sleep, he did as the angel of the Lord commanded him . . .

—Matthew 1:24

Joseph, in the worst time of his life, in the darkest moment, takes the problem upon himself, [even willing to be] accused in the eyes of the others in order to cover his bride. Joseph took his bride with him, saying: "I don't understand a thing, but the Lord told me this, and this one is going to appear as my son!" God puts us to the test. God saves us in the most difficult moments, because he is our Father. May the Lord enable us to understand this mystery of his journey with his people in history.

Homily, December 18, 2014

REFLECTION

When I face trials, do I trust that God will help me deal with them? In what ways can I entrust myself to the Lord?

PRAYER

Sometimes I don't understand why certain things happen in my life. Help me, Lord, to put myself into your hands with complete trust.

December 19

The New Creation

I will come praising the mighty deeds of the LORD GOD...

—Psalm 71:16

The Lord is capable of opening a new lineage, a new life: this is today's message. When humanity is exhausted, when it can no longer go forward, grace comes, and the Son comes, and salvation comes. That exhausted creation makes way for the new creation, and so we can call it a "re-creation." The truly marvelous miracle of creation leaves room for an even more marvelous miracle: re-creation, as the prayer says: "You, Lord, marvelously created the world, and even more marvelously recreated it. . . ." We await the newness of God. This is Christmas: the newness of God who remakes creation, all things, in a more marvelous way.

Homily, December 19, 2014

REFLECTION

In what ways has God been at work re-creating my life? If I sometimes feel exhausted by life, how can I find refreshment and peace?

PRAYER

Jesus, you said that if we take your yoke upon ourselves, we will find refreshment and peace. Help me to find the peace that you promise, so that at Christmas I will be ready to welcome you with a loving heart.

 December 20

Mary's Faith

Then Mary said, "Here am I, the servant of the Lord;
let it be with me according to your word."

—Luke 1:38

The attitude of Mary of Nazareth shows us that
being comes before *doing*, and *to leave the doing* to
God in order *to be* truly as he wants us. It is he who works
so many marvels in us. Mary is receptive, but not passive.
Because, on the physical level, she receives the power of
the Holy Spirit and then gives flesh and blood to the Son
of God who is formed within her. Thus, on the spiritual
level, she accepts the grace and corresponds to it with

faith. That is why Saint Augustine affirms that the Virgin "conceived in her heart before her womb" (*Discourses*, 215, 4).

Angelus, December 8, 2014

REFLECTION

How is my faith? In what ways can Mary's example of faith inspire my own following of the Lord?

PRAYER

Mary, my loving Mother, you never turn away anyone who comes to you. Present my requests to your Son, Jesus, and ask him to hear and answer my prayer.

Mary's Journey of Faith

In those days Mary set out and went with haste to a Judean town in the hill country . . .

—Luke 1:39

We also feel among us the living presence of the Virgin Mary. It is a motherly presence, a familial presence. . . . Love for Our Lady is one of the characteristics of popular devotion that must be respected and well directed. For this reason, I invite you to meditate on the last chapter of the Second Vatican Council's Constitution on the Church, *Lumen Gentium,* which speaks of Mary in the mystery of

Christ and of the Church. There it says that Mary "advanced in her pilgrimage of faith" (no. 58). Dear friends . . . I leave you this icon of Mary the pilgrim, who follows her Son Jesus and precedes us all in the journey of faith.

Regina Caeli Message, May 5, 2013

REFLECTION

How is my journey of faith going? How might I invite Mary to help me along the way, as she helped Elizabeth?

PRAYER

Mary, my mother, I trust in your loving intercession for me. Present to Jesus my needs and those of the whole world.

December 22

Hope Is Our Song

"He has come to the help of his servant Israel . . ."

—Luke 1:54

Hope is the virtue of those who, experiencing conflict—the struggle between life and death, good and evil—believe in the resurrection of Christ, in the victory of love. We heard the Song of Mary, the *Magnificat*; it is the song of hope, it is the song of the People of God walking through history. It is the song [of those who] . . . have faced the struggle of life while carrying in their hearts the hope of the little and the humble. . . . Do not allow yourselves to be robbed of hope. May we not be robbed of hope, because this strength is a grace, a gift from God which carries us forward with our eyes fixed on heaven. And Mary is always there, near those communities, our brothers and sisters. She accompanies them, suffers with them, and sings the *Magnificat* of hope with them.

Homily, August 15, 2013

REFLECTION

Advent is the season of hope. If I have been feeling down or discouraged lately, how can Mary help me in my struggles?

PRAYER

Intercede for me, Mary, and for all the troubled people of the world, that the hope of the coming Savior may carry us through the trials of life.

The Lord Is Near!

The Lord whom you seek will suddenly come to his temple.

—Malachi 3:1

With Our Lady and the Church, we would do well today to call out: "O Wisdom, O Key of David, O King of the Nations, come, come!" We would do well to repeat it many times. This prayer allows us to examine if our soul communicates to others that it does not wish to be disturbed, or if instead it is an open soul, a great soul ready to receive the Lord . . . a soul that already feels what the Church will tell us tomorrow in the antiphon:

Know that today the Lord comes and tomorrow you shall behold his glory!

Homily, December 23, 2013

REFLECTION

Our Advent journey is almost over. While I take care of last-minute preparations, how can I make some time for the Lord? Have I been to confession lately? If not, this is an opportune time.

PRAYER

Lord Jesus, I await your coming in grace on Christmas. Help me to welcome you with joy!

 December 24

O Emmanuel, Come to Deliver Us!

*"He has raised up a mighty savior for us
in the house of his servant David. . . ."*

—Luke 1:69

The grace which was revealed in our world is Jesus, born of the Virgin Mary, true man and true God. He has entered our history; he has shared our journey. He came to free us from darkness and to grant us light. In him was revealed the grace, the mercy, and the tender love of the Father; Jesus is Love incarnate. He is not simply a teacher of wisdom; he is not an ideal for which we strive while knowing that we are hopelessly distant from it. He is the meaning of life and history, who has pitched his tent in our midst.

Homily, December 24, 2013
(Midnight Mass)

REFLECTION

Our Advent journey is at an end. Tomorrow the joy of Christ's birth will light up the world. How will I welcome him?

PRAYER

Jesus, help me to rejoice at your birth! Thank you for coming into the world to be our Savior.

APPENDIX I

God Is with Us

The Humility of God

The people who walked in darkness
have seen a great light . . .

—Isaiah 9:2

Isaiah's prophecy announces the rising of a great light that breaks through the night. This light is born in Bethlehem and is welcomed by the loving arms of Mary, by the love of Joseph, by the wonder of the shepherds. . . . "This will be a sign for you: you will find a baby wrapped in swaddling clothes and lying in a manger" (Lk 2:12). The "sign" is in fact the humility of God, the humility of God taken to the extreme; it is the love with which, that night, he assumed our frailty, our suffering, our anxieties, our desires and our limitations. The message that everyone was expecting, that everyone was searching for in the depths of their souls, was none other than the tenderness of God—God who looks upon us with eyes full of love, who accepts our poverty; God who is in love with our smallness.

Homily, December 24, 2014 (Midnight Mass)

REFLECTION

Each Christmas, Jesus comes again into our hearts by grace. Yet he comes in humility. How is he coming to me today?

PRAYER

Lord Jesus, as I gaze on you in the manger, I am in awe at the love you have for each one of us. Help me to receive your love and radiate it to others.

 The Holy Family

Peace and Joy in Family Life

As God's chosen ones, holy and beloved, clothe your-
selves with compassion, kindness, humility, meekness,
and patience.

—Colossians 3:12

Today our gaze on the Holy Family lets us also be drawn into the simplicity of the life they led in Nazareth. It is an example that does our families great good, helping them increasingly to become communities of love and reconciliation, in which tenderness, mutual help, and mutual forgiveness is experienced. Let us remember the three key phrases for living in peace and joy in the family: "may I," "thank you," and "sorry." In our family, when we are not intrusive and ask, "may I"; in our family when we are not selfish and learn to say, "thank you"; and when in a family one realizes he has done something wrong and knows how to say, "sorry"— then in that family there is peace and joy.

Angelus, December 29, 2013

REFLECTION

Every family has its struggles and difficulties. How do I deal with these? How can I act with greater love for all of my family members?

PRAYER

Jesus, when you came to dwell among us, you did so by living in a family. Help me to imitate your example of faithful love and mercy toward all, but especially toward my family.

Mother and Son

But Mary treasured all these words and pondered them in her heart.

—Luke 2:19

In addition to contemplating God's face, we can also praise him and glorify him, like the shepherds who came away from Bethlehem with a song of thanksgiving after seeing the Child and his young mother (see Lk 2:16). The two were together, just as they were together at Calvary, because *Christ and his mother are inseparable.* There is a very close relationship between them, as there is between every child and his or her mother. The flesh (*caro*) of Christ—which, as Tertullian says, is the hinge (*cardo*) of our salvation—was knit together in the womb of Mary (see Ps 139:13). This inseparability is also clear from the fact that Mary, chosen beforehand to be the Mother of the Redeemer, shared intimately in his entire mission, remaining at her Son's side to the end on Calvary.

Homily, January 1, 2015

REFLECTION

When the shepherds looked for Jesus, they found him with Mary, his mother. It is the same today. Those who find Mary will find Jesus, for her role is to lead us to him.

PRAYER

Mary, my mother, lead me to a deeper knowledge and love of your son, Jesus.

 The Epiphany

The Magi and the Star

When they saw that the star had stopped, they were
overwhelmed with joy.

—Matthew 2:10

The example of the Magi helps us to lift our gaze
toward the star and to follow the great desires of
our heart. They teach us not to be content with a life of
mediocrity, of "playing it safe," but to let ourselves be
attracted always by what is good, true, and beautiful . . .
by God, who is all of this, and so much more! And they
teach us not to be deceived by appearances, by what the
world considers great, wise, and powerful. . . . Today this

is of vital importance: to keep the faith. We must press on farther . . . toward Bethlehem, where, in the simplicity of a dwelling on the outskirts . . . there shines forth the Sun from on high, the King of the universe. By the example of the Magi, with our little lights, may we seek the Light and keep the faith.

Homily, January 6, 2014

REFLECTION

What "star" do I seek most in life? Is Jesus the guiding star that I look to at all times?

PRAYER

Jesus, thank you for coming to earth to save us from sin. I want to follow you and to model my life on yours. Give me the grace to be your faithful disciple.

APPENDIX II

Prayers of Pope Francis

1

Prayer to the Immaculate

Virgin most holy and immaculate,
    to you, the honor of our people
and the loving protector of our city,
do we turn with loving trust.

You are all-beautiful, O Mary!
In you there is no sin.
Awaken in all of us a renewed desire for holiness.
May the splendor of truth shine forth in our words,
the song of charity resound in our works,
purity and chastity abide in our hearts and bodies,
and the full beauty of the Gospel be evident in
    our lives.

You are all-beautiful, O Mary!
In you the Word of God became flesh.
Help us always to heed the Lord's voice.
May we never be indifferent to the cry of the poor,

or untouched by the sufferings of the sick and those
   in need;
may we be sensitive to the loneliness of the elderly
   and the vulnerability of children,
and always love and cherish the life of every
   human being.

You are all-beautiful, O Mary!
In you is the fullness of joy born of life with God.
Help us never to forget the meaning of our earthly
   journey.
May the kindly light of faith illumine our days,
the comforting power of hope direct our steps,
the contagious warmth of love stir our hearts,
and may our gaze be fixed on God, in whom true
   joy is found.

You are all-beautiful, O Mary!
Hear our prayer, graciously hear our plea.
May the beauty of God's merciful love in Jesus abide
   in our hearts;
and may this divine beauty save us, our city, and the
entire world. Amen.

*On the occasion of the Solemnity
of the Immaculate Conception (December 8, 2013)*

Prayer to the Holy Family

Jesus, Mary, and Joseph,
   in you we contemplate the splendor of true love.
To you we turn with trust.
Holy Family of Nazareth, grant that our families,
   too, may be places of communion and prayer,
authentic schools of the Gospel,
and small domestic churches.
Holy Family of Nazareth, may families never again
experience violence, rejection, and division;
may all who have been hurt or scandalized
find ready comfort and healing.
Holy Family of Nazareth,
make us once more mindful
of the sacredness and inviolability of the family
and its beauty in God's plan.
Jesus, Mary, and Joseph, graciously hear our prayer.

Angelus, December 29, 2013

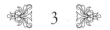

3

Prayer to Mary, Woman of Listening

Mary, woman of listening, open our ears; grant us to know how to listen to the word of your Son, Jesus, among the thousands of words of this world. Grant that we may listen to the reality in which we live, to every person we encounter, especially those who are poor, in need, in hardship.

Mary, woman of decision, illuminate our mind and our heart so that we may obey, unhesitatingly, the word of your Son, Jesus. Give us the courage to decide, not to let ourselves be dragged along, letting others direct our life.

Mary, woman of action, obtain that our hands and feet move "with haste" toward others, to bring them the charity and love of your Son, Jesus, to bring the light of the Gospel to the world, as you did. Amen.

Prayer to Mary at the conclusion of the recital of the Holy Rosary (Saint Peter's Square, May 31, 2013)

4

Prayer to Mary, Mother of the Church and Mother of Our Faith

Mother, help our faith! Open our ears to hear God's word and to recognize his voice and call. Awaken in us a desire to follow in his footsteps, to go forth from our own land, and to receive his promise.

Help us to be touched by his love, that we may touch him in faith. Help us to entrust ourselves fully to him and to believe in his love, especially at times of trial, beneath the shadow of the cross, when our faith is called to mature. Sow in our faith the joy of the Risen One.

Remind us that those who believe are never alone.

Teach us to see all things with the eyes of Jesus, that he may be light for our path. And may this light of faith always increase in us, until the dawn of that undying day, which is Christ himself, your Son, our Lord!

Prayer at the conclusion of the encyclical
Lumen Fidei, *June 29, 2013*

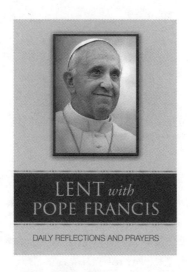

Lent with Pope Francis

Daily Reflections and Prayers

*Compiled and with reflection questions and prayers
by Donna Giaimo, FSP*

Lent with Pope Francis offers inspiration for each day of
Lent from the Pope's homilies, public addresses, and
other writings.

Paperback, 128 pages
0-8198-4572-8   978-0-8198-4572-6
 $7.95 USD

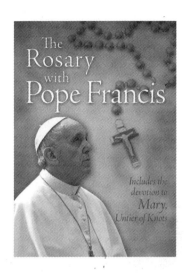

The Rosary with Pope Francis

*Compiled and with an Introduction
by Marianne Lorraine Trouvé, FSP*

This book offers the insightful words of Pope Francis for each Hail Mary, using quotes from the Holy Father's various homilies, addresses, and written texts.

Paperback, 112 pages
0-8198-6500-1   978-0-8198-6500-7
$9.95 USD

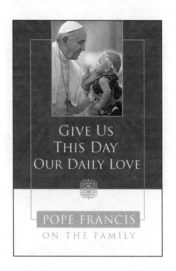

GIVE US
THIS DAY
OUR DAILY LOVE

POPE FRANCIS
ON THE FAMILY

Give Us This Day Our Daily Love

Pope Francis on the Family

*Compiled by Theresa Aletheia Noble, FSP
and Donna Giaimo, FSP*

In his direct and delightful style, Pope Francis offers families a banquet of encouragement; inspiration; and wise, practical advice.

Paperback, 192 pages
0-8198-3135-2   978-0-8198-3135-4
$12.95 USD

BOOKS & MEDIA

A mission of the Daughters of St. Paul

As apostles of Jesus Christ, evangelizing today's world:

We are CALLED to holiness
by God's living Word and Eucharist.

We COMMUNICATE the Gospel message
through our lives and through all
available forms of media.

We SERVE the Church
by responding to the hopes and needs
of all people with the Word of God,
in the spirit of St. Paul.

For more information visit our website:
www.pauline.org.

Pauline
BOOKS & MEDIA

The Daughters of St. Paul operate book and media centers at the following addresses. Visit, call or write the one nearest you today, or find us at www.pauline.org.

CALIFORNIA

3908 Sepulveda Blvd, Culver City, CA 90230   310-397-8676

935 Brewster Avenue, Redwood City, CA 94063   650-369-4230

5945 Balboa Avenue, San Diego, CA 92111   858-565-9181

FLORIDA

145 S.W. 107th Avenue, Miami, FL 33174   305-559-6715

HAWAII

1143 Bishop Street, Honolulu, HI 96813   808-521-2731

ILLINOIS

172 North Michigan Avenue, Chicago, IL 60601   312-346-4228

LOUISIANA

4403 Veterans Memorial Blvd, Metairie, LA 70006   504-887-7631

MASSACHUSETTS

885 Providence Hwy, Dedham, MA 02026   781-326-5385

MISSOURI

9804 Watson Road, St. Louis, MO 63126   314-965-3512

NEW YORK

64 W. 38th Street, New York, NY 10018   212-754-1110

SOUTH CAROLINA

243 King Street, Charleston, SC 29401   843-577-0175

TEXAS

Currently no book center; for parish exhibits or outreach evangelization, contact: 210–488–4123 or SanAntonio@paulinemedia.com

VIRGINIA

1025 King Street, Alexandria, VA 22314   703-549-3806

CANADA

3022 Dufferin Street, Toronto, ON M6B 3T5   416-781-9131

¡También somos su fuente para libros,
videos y música en español!